E

Resources for Multilingual Writers and ESL

A Hacker Handbooks Supplement

Marcy Carbajal Van Horn
St. Edward's University

BEDFORD / ST. MARTIN'S   BOSTON ◆ NEW YORK

Manufactured in the United States of America.

6   5   4   3   2   1
f   e   d   c   b   a

For information, write: Bedford/St. Martin's, 75 Arlington Street, Boston, MA 02116   (617-399-4000)

ISBN-10: 0-312-65685-8
ISBN-13: 978-0-312-65685-0

ACKNOWLEDGMENTS

Averil Coxhead, excerpt from sublist 1 of "A New Academic Word List" published
    in *TESOL Quarterly* 34. Copyright 2000. Reprinted with permission.
Rebecca Webber, "Make Your Own Luck." *Psychology Today*, May/June 2010,
    excerpts from pages 63–68. Copyright © 2010 by Sussex Publishers, LLC.
    Reprinted by permission of *Psychology Today.*

E

Resources for Multilingual Writers and ESL

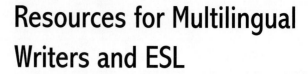

E Resources for Multilingual Writers and ESL

No matter what your educational background is, entering a college environment will provide opportunities for new ways of doing things. Even if you speak English fluently, you may find college intimidating at first. Sections E1–E4 focus on ways to make your transition to college smooth and successful.

E1 Understanding college-level expectations

In the United States, college classrooms are interactive—students are expected to participate in discussions and sometimes work together in groups. Students are also treated as adults who are responsible for managing their own course work and schedule. Succeeding in this environment may require you to adjust your habits both inside and outside the classroom.

E1-a Read your syllabus carefully.

At the beginning of the semester, your instructor will give you a syllabus, a document that provides critical information about the course, including assignments, grading policies, and your instructor's contact information. (For a sample syllabus, see p. E-4.) Be sure to read through your syllabus carefully so that you understand your instructor's expectations; refer to it often during the term. College students are usually expected to keep up with the course work outlined in a syllabus without reminders from their instructor.

When you look at the syllabi for all your courses, you may find that you have several major assignments due on the same day. You may also have smaller assignments that overlap. A calendar or schedule program can help you keep track of the due dates for all your classes. It is a good idea to check your syllabus or your calendar regularly, especially before each class session, to remind yourself of readings and other assignments.

E1-b Understand classroom expectations in the United States.

Education is a cultural activity, and classroom emphases and expectations vary across the globe. In the United States, college students are expected to show critical thinking. In other words, college instructors expect their students not just to memorize information but to ask questions, challenge assumptions, see patterns, and apply knowledge.

SAMPLE SYLLABUS

ENG 1101: College Composition I

Instructor: Dr. Morgan Felix

Phone: (321) 234-5678

E-mail address: mfelix@yourcollege.edu

① **Office:** Anderson Hall, room 312-B

Office hours: Monday, Wednesday, and Friday, 1:00-2:30 p.m., or by appointment

Course Description

College Composition I (ENG 1101) is designed to give you training and practice in developing literacy in academic English. In this course, you will read and analyze academic texts, and you will write about those texts with an analytical purpose. Multiple drafts are expected for each writing assignment.

Course Objectives

1. Students will learn that writing is a process that requires planning, drafting, revising, peer reviewing, and editing.
2. Students will be competent in reading and analyzing college-level texts.
3. Students will be competent in structuring essays appropriate for college courses, using standard English conventions.

② Required Textbooks

Kennedy, X. J., Dorothy M. Kennedy, and Jane E. Aaron. *The Bedford Reader*. 10th ed. Boston: Bedford, 2009.
Hacker, Diana, and Nancy Sommers. *A Writer's Reference*. 7th ed. Boston: Bedford, 2011.

Grading System

Your final grade will be based on the following:
- Take-home essays, including drafts = 60%
- In-class (timed) essays = 20%

③ - Attendance and participation = 10%
- Final exam = 10%

Schedule of Readings and Assignments

You are required to complete the assigned readings *before* each class. Major assignments are listed in **bold**.

④
  BR = Reading assignments from *The Bedford Reader*
  AWR = Reading assignments from *A Writer's Reference*

SAMPLE SYLLABUS (continued)

Week	Day	Class topics	Readings/ assignments due
1	Tu	Introduction to the course/syllabus	
	Th	In-class diagnostic essay	
2	Tu	Writing description essays	*BR*: pages 137-83 *AWR*: C1 and C2 ⑤
	Th	Essay 1 workshop (focus on global revisions)	Essay 1, draft 1 due *AWR*: C3-a to C3-c
3	Tu	Essay 1 workshop (focus on editing)	Essay 1, draft 2 due *AWR*: C3-d
	Th	Strategies for taking essay tests	**Essay 1 final draft due** ⑥

① Instructors want to talk to their students. Often they list contact information and office hours on the course syllabus.

② A syllabus often includes a list of materials to purchase.

③ Most instructors expect students to participate in class. Participation is often part of the final grade.

④ Abbreviations used in the schedule are explained.

⑤ Readings for each class period are listed in the right-hand column.

⑥ Major deadlines are listed in bold.

Students might learn their course material in the following ways:

- by participating in class discussions
- by learning rules, patterns, and theories and then demonstrating how they relate to a variety of situations
- by synthesizing (connecting) ideas from multiple sources
- by working with others to develop new approaches or hypotheses

While you might sometimes be required to memorize or learn basic facts and principles, your instructors will most often expect you to move beyond memorization and show critical thinking about the content of the course. The following examples are questions from exams in introductory economics classes. The first example is from a class that emphasizes memorization of facts; the second is from a class in which students are expected to apply concepts to everyday situations.

EMPHASIS ON MEMORIZATION

QUESTION   What does "opportunity cost" mean?

ANSWER   "Opportunity cost" is the value of a resource measured in terms of the next-best alternative use of that resource.

EMPHASIS ON CRITICAL THINKING

QUESTION/TASK   Illustrate the concept of "opportunity cost" with an example from your own life.

ANSWER   The opportunity cost of going to the movies with my roommate last night was the extra time I could otherwise have spent studying for my economics exam. In other words, I gave up extra study time by going to the movies.

To answer the second question, students needed to learn the definition of *opportunity cost*. But they were expected to go beyond the definition and show critical thinking by applying the definition to their own example.

E1-c Participate actively in class and in groups.

Because US colleges value creativity and originality, instructors expect students (especially in smaller classes or sections) to participate in class—to share their ideas about the course material, to work together in groups, and sometimes even to lead class discussions. Because students' contributions are so highly valued, many instructors devote a portion of the final course grade to "class participation."

Class participation

To increase your chances of success, take an active part in class discussions. Remember that your instructors will not always expect you to recall or restate an idea from the text or a previous class. More often, they will ask you to show critical thinking (see E1-b). If you do not participate, your instructor might assume that you don't know the material or that you have come to class unprepared.

If you feel intimidated by class discussions, you can often overcome your fears by preparing well before class. Here are some strategies you can use to get ready for class discussions:

- Actively read and annotate the assigned textbook pages or articles before class. Highlight or underline major ideas, and write

notes or questions in the margins of the page. (See the sections
on active reading and annotating texts in your handbook.)

- Anticipate some of the questions your instructor might ask in
class. Many instructors provide discussion topics or reading
questions in the syllabus or in assignments.

- When you finish your assigned reading, write down some of your
thoughts about the text in your journal or notebook. Using just a
few sentences, try to summarize the main points of the passage.
Reflect on the importance of these main ideas. How do they
relate to other topics you have discussed in class?

- Just before class, review your notes so that you can share your
ideas when the discussion begins.

Working in groups

Group work, or collaborative activity, gives students the chance to
learn about the assigned course work while building communication
and leadership skills.

A group project for an environmental studies course, for example, might require students to learn about and report on the levels of
chemicals in the local water supply. To complete the project, the team
will need to take several steps:

- Determine what tasks need to be completed to find answers to
their questions

- Divide the work among the team members

- Choose a leader (or leaders) to coordinate the team's actions

- Work together to write, compile, and edit the final report

The group's final report on the water supply will include contributions
from all group members, much more information than a person working alone could gather.

You might find it difficult to adjust to collaborative work if you
come from a culture that emphasizes individual learning or if your
high school teachers did not assign group projects. But be prepared
to encounter group work in college. Most instructors feel that it cre-
ates an atmosphere in which new ideas can emerge. It also serves as
preparation for the professional world, where many jobs require some
form of collaborative activity.

Showing respect for your peers

While instructors may encourage you to give your own interpretations
of material, to argue a point using information in the textbook, or to

apply critical thinking to basic concepts, remember that most instructors expect you to respect your peers' ideas. In some cultures, it may be appropriate to challenge individuals directly by saying that they are wrong or by exposing their personal flaws. In the United States, however, directly challenging a classmate in this manner is considered rude and inappropriate. If you disagree with someone's opinion, it is often best to state that you disagree with the idea—not with the person who said it—and then to explain your reasons with evidence or examples. Likewise, you should state your own opinions and interpretations in a reasonable tone and expect that other students will want to discuss your ideas or even to politely disagree. (See the chart on p. E-9.)

Speaking in English

The ability to speak two or more languages is an asset that you should take pride in, but it is also important to be sensitive to your instructor and classmates in your shared learning environment. Whenever possible, use the language that all participants in the class can understand easily. In US academic settings, this language is English. If you need to discuss or explain an idea in your native language with one of your classmates, be sure to alert your instructor first. If you begin speaking to a friend in a language your instructor does not understand, your instructor may think that you are not paying attention (which is considered rude). Try to think of the class time as a regular opportunity to practice your spoken English.

E1-d Attend classes regularly; arrive a few minutes before each class begins.

Attending class regularly is important for success. Attending class will both reinforce the material that you have studied on your own and provide you with additional opportunities for language practice. You'll have to listen to your instructor and classmates and participate in the discussion. You'll also have to practice reading what your instructor writes on the board (or displays on a screen) and practice writing by taking notes. The classroom experience provides valuable repetition of key ideas and important facts that you will most likely have to recall or apply on tests and assignments.

Your instructors will expect you to arrive at each class a few minutes before the period begins so the discussion can start at the

Showing respect in class discussions

Inappropriate	Appropriate
▪ You're wrong.	▪ I can see your point, but I disagree because. . . .
▪ That's a stupid idea.	▪ I understand what you mean, but can you back it up?
▪ You don't know what you're talking about.	▪ You make a good point, but there are other ideas to consider. For example, . . .

scheduled time. Make a habit of arriving about five minutes before class begins, and use the time to scan your textbook or review your notes from the previous class or from your reading. It is usually much easier to follow the class discussion—especially if your listening skills are not yet fluent—when you review the material first.

E1-e Get extra help when necessary.

If you have questions about the course material or problems with an assignment, do not be afraid to seek extra help from your instructor or others at your school.

Writing centers

Most colleges have writing centers (sometimes called *writing labs*) staffed with instructors or experienced students, often called *writing tutors* or *consultants*. They can assist you at various stages of the writing process. The tutors are typically trained to help in the following areas:

- brainstorming ideas for a writing assignment
- suggesting ways to revise a draft
- identifying areas of a draft that need clarification
- pointing out places in a draft where more development is needed
- diagnosing repetitive mistakes in a paper

It is important to remember that writing center tutors provide guidance, not proofreading services. With their help, you can learn to analyze assignments and evaluate your own writing. They are not

Visiting the writing center

Step 1: Gather your materials.

- Gather any materials your instructor has provided: the assignment, sample papers, your syllabus.
- Gather your own materials: a printout of your essay draft; copies of texts you have cited in your paper; previous papers with instructor comments and grades.

Step 2: Organize your materials and prepare questions.

- Read over the assignment carefully to understand it. If you are confused, ask your instructor to clarify the assignment before you visit the writing center.
- Look at previous papers with instructor comments. Can any of those comments help you revise your current paper?
- Create a list of questions about your draft, noting a few issues to focus your time with the tutor—places where you aren't sure of a phrase or a verb or where you need help thinking through an idea.

Step 3: Check the writing center's Web site for policies and procedures.

- Find out where the writing center is located and when it's open.
- Make an appointment, if one is required.
- Get tips on what to bring to your writing center session.
- Find out if there is a limit to the number of appointments you can make or the number of drafts you can review with a tutor.
- Check for tutors who are specially trained to assist multilingual students.

Step 4: Visit the writing center.

- Be on time and treat your tutor with courtesy and respect.
- Participate actively by asking questions and taking notes.
- Understand the limitations of your visit. In most cases, you should expect to cover one or two major issues. The tutor will probably not have time to review your entire paper—unless it is very short.
- Understand the tutor's role. Most tutors are trained to give you tips and suggestions, but they will not write or edit your paper for you. They will encourage you to take notes or make revisions.

Step 5: Reflect on your visit.

- As soon as possible after your visit, write down anything you didn't have time to write during the session and clarify any notes you took so that you understand them when you revise your paper.

- Use your notes to review your entire paper for the problems you and the tutor discussed. Don't focus only on the examples you looked at in the session.
- Do not feel obligated to follow advice that you disagree with or are not comfortable following. Tutors are trained to provide you with feedback and suggestions, but you are the author; you decide which changes will help you accurately express your meaning.
- As you clarify your notes and revise, keep track of other questions or goals for the next writing center visit.

there just to "fix" your mistakes. The more prepared you are for your visit and the more willing you are to discuss your writing problems, the more productive your time with the tutor will be.

Before you visit the writing center, think about specific problems you are having with your assignment. Maybe you don't know what the assignment is asking you to do. Maybe you have a lot of sources but don't know how to organize them. Maybe you're stuck on one paragraph. Make a list of specific problems, and try to organize them into several questions you can ask the tutor. Bring materials related to your assignment to show the tutor as useful background: the assignment itself, an outline if you've done one, notes, drafts, and source materials. Be prepared to discuss your writing actively—to ask the tutor questions and to respond to questions the tutor asks you.

The chart on pages E-10 and E-11 can help you prepare for a visit to the writing center.

Instructor's office hours

In some cultures, visiting an instructor's office may be considered disrespectful. However, instructors in the United States usually encourage students to visit them during their office hours. Check your course syllabus to determine when your instructor is available. If you are confused by an assignment or uncertain about any course material, don't be afraid to ask your instructor for help.

Helpful Web sites

Many online writing centers and ESL Web sites provide helpful information and exercises for practice. Here are a few of them.

- *Activities for ESL Students*
  http://a4esl.org
  This site, sponsored by the *Internet TESL Journal*, provides quizzes, tests, exercises, and puzzles submitted by ESL teachers.

- *Dave's ESL Cafe*
  http://www.eslcafe.com
  This well-known site offers several resources for students: grammar lessons, quizzes, and a discussion board where you can post questions and receive advice from students and teachers around the world.
- *Guide to Grammar and Writing*
  http://grammar.ccc.commnet.edu/grammar
  Using clear examples and detailed explanations, this site includes comprehensive coverage of everything from punctuation to research. It also includes quizzes on various grammar and writing issues.
- *Randall's ESL Cyber Listening Lab*
  http://esl-lab.com
  This site has a wide variety of exercises—from the everyday to the academic—that provide audio files for listening and quizzes to test understanding.
- *Voice of America: Wordmaster*
  http://voanews.com/specialenglish/wordmaster/index.cfm
  This news and information site allows users to read along as they listen to audio files of articles about English grammar and usage. The site also includes word games and quizzes.

Web sites and URLs often change; for the most up-to-date information, go to hackerhandbooks.com/writersref and check the Multilingual/ESL section.

E2 Strategies for improving your academic English

Few residents of the United States speak academic English in all situations every day. Most of us regularly speak an informal variety: We speak in sentence fragments, we use slang, and we use regional forms. However, we should use academic English when we want to reach broader audiences—particularly in college or business settings.

As you aim to improve your performance in academic English, you might need to broaden your range of strategies. You might try a number of reading or listening activities, for example, or make an effort to practice with more grammar exercises. You may decide to

formal and informal English • practice • reading • listening •
talking • exercises • spoken English • recognizing written words

E2-b

E-13

consult a dictionary or a thesaurus more regularly or to keep a vocabulary notebook. Such strategies provide practice that can help you gain familiarity with academic English.

E2-a Engage in intensive and extensive language activities.

Languages—including academic English—are learned through intensive and extensive practice. Intensive practice involves focusing on a small amount of material with a high level of attention. Completing grammar exercises, for instance, is an intensive activity. A grammar exercise will help you develop control over a very specific grammatical concept, such as past-tense verbs or the use of prepositions following adjectives.

Extensive practice involves absorbing a larger quantity of information, typically over a longer period of time. Extensive practices focus less on individual words or forms and more on general comprehension and fluency—your ability to understand, use, and think in English without translating from your native language. Listening to the radio for general understanding is an extensive practice that can help you develop your speed and your grasp of "natural" English forms in various contexts.

The chart on page E-14 gives some everyday examples of intensive and extensive language activities. (Section E4-b provides a list of writing prompts that can be used for both intensive and extensive practice.)

E2-b Read while listening.

If you learned English informally (through conversation rather than in a classroom) or if your middle school and high school classes did not cover English grammar thoroughly, you may need to pay special attention to the differences between spoken English and academic written English. The skills you use when speaking English are different from those you use when writing English. You need to train your *ears* to know what sounds natural, but you also have to train your *eyes* to know what standard English forms look like.

If you speak English well but are having trouble using standard forms or correct English spelling when you write, you might practice reading and listening at the same time. Most libraries carry audio

Sample activities for intensive and extensive language practice

Reading

Intensive	Extensive
▪ reading a textbook chapter for content	▪ reading novels or nonfiction books for pleasure
▪ reading difficult material with unfamiliar vocabulary	▪ reading newspapers or magazines regularly
▪ reading essays to understand different organizational styles or grammatical patterns	▪ reading Web sites or blogs for entertainment

Writing

Intensive	Extensive
▪ writing an essay for class or for a test	▪ e-mailing friends, instant messaging, blogging
▪ writing a formal letter, application, or résumé	▪ keeping a journal or diary regularly
▪ completing exercises that focus on specific grammatical concepts	▪ freewriting or fiction writing for enjoyment

Listening

Intensive	Extensive
▪ listening to take notes or to follow directions (in class)	▪ listening to friends talk
▪ listening to dictation to record text accurately	▪ listening to TV shows or movies
▪ listening for specific words, sounds, or intonations	▪ listening to the radio

Speaking

Intensive	Extensive
▪ giving a formal speech	▪ having a conversation with English-speaking friends
▪ practicing careful pronunciation	▪ chatting on the phone
▪ emphasizing or focusing on specific grammatical forms (such as the past tense) while speaking	▪ participating in class discussions

books, and some libraries even package the paper books and audio books together. If you read a book while you listen to the audio version of the book, you can begin to connect the visual forms with words you have already heard before. If you purchase a paper copy of the book, you can also underline or highlight new words—or words that look different from the way they sound—while you listen. After finishing a few pages or a chapter, stop the audio and review the new forms you've marked. Combined reading and listening practice can help you understand standard English forms and use them in your own writing.

The following Web sites provide text and audio—you can listen to someone speak the words as you read along.

- *American Rhetoric*
  http://www.americanrhetoric.com
  Hear famous American speeches while you read the text. Some speeches are also available in video.
- *American Stories on VOA Special English*
  http://www1.voanews.com/learningenglish/programs
  Listen to and read short stories by American authors.
- *Poets.org Audio and Video*
  http://www.poets.org/page.php/prmID/361
  Listen to well-known poets read their own works as you read along.
- *VOA Special English News Radio for English Learners*
  http://www1.voanews.com/learningenglish/home
  Listen to current global news (broadcast by the US government) while reading the text.

E2-c Use an English-English dictionary or a thesaurus designed for multilingual writers.

Many students who learn English in their home country before coming to the United States use bilingual dictionaries, which list words in English with native-language translations or vice versa. By now, you have probably noticed that some words in these dictionaries have conversational translations that are not appropriate for academic work. While the dictionaries can help you understand what you read and may help beginning writers, they are not always the best resource for college writing.

For help with understanding and using college-level vocabulary, consider investing in an English-English dictionary that is designed for multilingual writers. These dictionaries typically provide both definitions and sample sentences for each word. Many also provide information that is not in dictionaries for native speakers. For example, they usually note whether a noun is count, noncount, or both, and they often provide information about a word's level of formality. The following are some dictionaries and thesauri (books that provide lists of synonyms, words with similar meanings) designed for multilingual writers.

DICTIONARIES

- *Cambridge Advanced Learner's Dictionary*
- *Collin's COBUILD Advanced Learner's English Dictionary*
- *Longman Advanced American Dictionary*
- *Oxford ESL Dictionary for Students of American English*
- *Random House Webster's Dictionary of American English: ESL / Learner's Edition*

THESAURI

- *Longman's Language Activator*
- *Webster's New Explorer Thesaurus*

E2-d Become familiar with the Academic Word List.

If most of your English instruction and practice so far have focused on English for conversational situations (such as traveling, shopping, giving and asking for directions, narrating daily activities, and sharing explanations or personal stories), you might feel overwhelmed by the terms you find in your academic reading and in class discussions. You might feel that your own English vocabulary needs to grow before you can fully express your academic knowledge in writing.

Although it is possible—and often preferable—to learn academic vocabulary in the context of your readings and class discussions, you can get a head start by becoming familiar with the words in the Academic Word List. The Academic Word List, compiled by a linguist, contains almost six hundred of the most frequently used academic English words. (The chart on p. E-17 presents the sixty most commonly used words; you can find the complete list online at the URL in the chart.)

Because you will encounter these words regularly in textbooks and in class, it's a good idea to familiarize yourself with them early in your college experience.

dictionary • thesaurus • academic vocabulary •
word beginnings (*non-*, *pre-*, etc.) • word endings (*-dom*, *-able*, etc.)

E2-e   E-17

Academic Word List

analyze	define	indicate	proceed
approach	derive	individual	process
area	distribute	interpret	require
assess	economy	involve	research
assume	environment	issue	respond
authority	establish	labor	role
available	estimate	legal	section
benefit	evident	legislate	sector
concept	export	major	significant
consist	factor	method	similar
constitute	finance	occur	source
context	formula	percent	specific
contract	function	period	structure
create	identify	policy	theory
data	income	principle	vary

Source: Averil Coxhead, "A New Academic Word List," *TESOL Quarterly* 34 (2000): 213–38, app. A, sublist 1. The entire Academic Word List is available at http://www.victoria.ac.nz/lals/resources /academicwordlist.

E2-e Learn how prefixes and suffixes affect a word's meaning.

A prefix is added to the beginning of a word to expand or change the word's core meaning (its *root* or *stem*). The prefix *non-*, for instance, added to the root word *toxic* changes the meaning of the word from "poisonous" to "not poisonous." The chart on pages E-18 and E-19 will help you become familiar with some common prefixes, their meanings, and some words in which you might encounter them.

Suffixes are word endings that indicate a word's part of speech (noun, verb, adjective, adverb, and so on). The chart on pages E-19 and E-20 can help you learn how a word's suffix determines its part of speech. (For descriptions of the parts of speech, see the basic grammar section of your handbook.)

Consider the English noun *democracy*, for example, which has many related forms: *democrat* (a noun), *democratize* (a verb), *democratic* (an adjective), and *democratically* (an adverb). If you were to switch any of these two words in a sentence, your readers might become confused:

▶ We live in a ~~democratic.~~ democracy.

Prefixes and their meanings

Prefix	Basic meaning	Examples
a-, an-	without, not	apolitical (not political); anaerobic (without oxygen)
ante-	before	antecedent (an element that comes before something); antebellum (before war, particularly the US Civil War)
anti-	against	antibiotic (medicine that works against bacteria); antiwar (against war)
auto-	self	autobiography (biography of oneself); automatic (self-acting)
bi-	two	biannual (occurring every two years); bicultural (being part of two cultures)
co-, col-, com-, con-, cor-	together, with	coincide (happen together); collaborate (work with); commiserate (be unhappy together); congregate (assemble together); correspond (communicate with)
dis-	opposite, not	disagree (not agree); disappear (opposite of appear)
ex-	out, former	exclude (keep out); ex-president (former president)
il-, im-, in-, ir-	not	illegal (not legal); impatient (not patient); incompatible (not compatible); irresponsible (not responsible)
inter-	between	international (between countries)
intra-, intro-	within, inward	intracultural (within one culture); introspective (reflecting, looking within oneself)
intro-	in, into	introduce (bring in)
mis-	wrong, bad	mislead (lead someone in the wrong direction); misuse (use wrongly)
mono-	single, only	monopoly (control by one person or group); monotheism (belief in one God)
non-	not, without	nonverbal (without speech); nontraditional (not traditional)
omni-	all	omnivorous (eating all foods)

Prefix	Basic meaning	Examples
pan-	all	panacea (cure for all diseases); pantheon (temple of all gods)
poly-	many	polygamy (marriage to more than one person at one time); polyglot (a person who speaks many languages)
post-	after, later	postmodern (after the modern period); postpone (put off till later)
pre-	before	prejudice (judgment before sufficient knowledge); preseason (before the season)
pro-	forward	proceed (go forward)
re-	again	reappear (appear again); redo (do again)
sub-	under	submarine (underwater vessel); subway (underground train)
super-	over, more than, huge	superimpose (place something over another); superpower (huge power)
un-	opposite, not	unimportant (not important)

Suffixes and their parts of speech

Nouns

Suffix	Examples
-acy	aristocracy, democracy, privacy, supremacy
-ance, -ence	assistance, dependence, independence, science
-ancy, -ency	infancy, vacancy, delinquency, emergency
-dom	boredom, freedom, kingdom, wisdom
-er, -or	computer, stapler, writer, counselor
-hood	childhood, motherhood, neighborhood
-ism	Buddhism, communism, journalism, perfectionism
-ist	chemist, dermatologist, pianist, socialist
-ity, -ety, -ty	unity, society, variety, liberty
-ment	enjoyment, government, replacement

→

Suffixes and their parts of speech (continued)

Suffix	Examples
-ness	forgetfulness, goodness, happiness, sadness
-ship	courtship, friendship, membership, partnership
-sion, -tion, -ion	admission, immigration, pollution, vacation

Verbs

Suffix	Examples
-ate	anticipate, complicate, cooperate, reiterate
-ify	amplify, mystify, quantify, terrify
-ize	computerize, demonize, maximize, publicize

Adjectives

Suffix	Examples
-able, -ible	drinkable, forgivable, edible, legible
-al	functional, legal, physical, visual
-ent, -ient	obedient, salient, sentient, silent
-ful	beautiful, hopeful, powerful, regretful
-ic	automatic, egocentric, poetic, systematic
-ive	active, extensive, passive, productive
-less	fruitless, harmless, homeless, useless
-ous, -ious	delicious, delirious, gracious, mysterious

Adverbs

Suffix	Examples
-ly	easily, convincingly, hopefully, quickly

E2-f Keep a vocabulary notebook.

Use a vocabulary notebook to keep track of new words—especially those that you have seen more than one time or that you have seen in a few different places. While you are reading for your classes, jot down a few new words in your notebook, along with the sentences in which you found the words. After you finish reading, look up each word in an English-English dictionary (see E2-c). Record the word's definition and part of speech, and scan the dictionary page for related words. If you look up the noun *effect*, for instance, you will find in the

RESOURCES See the following section of your handbook's companion Web site:
> Multilingual/ESL > Blank vocabulary notebook pages

word endings (*-dom*, *-able*, etc.) • taking notes • new words •
grammar errors • example sentences • written and spoken skills

E2-h

E-21

SAMPLE VOCABULARY NOTEBOOK ENTRY

Word: *civilized*	**Form: Noun Verb (Adj.) Adv.**
	Other _____
Meaning:	**Related words:**
Sophisticated, developed	*civil (adj.)*
	civilize (v., transitive)
	civilian (n., person)
	civilization (n.)
Sentence: *The Romans believed that the Germanic tribes from the north were not <u>civilized</u>.*	

same entry or on the same page the verb *effect*, the related adjective *effective*, the noun *effectiveness*, and the adverb *effectively*. Keeping track of related words is an easy way to expand your vocabulary with little effort. See the sample vocabulary notebook entry above.

E2-g Keep an editing log.

As part of the writing process, you will read and reread your own writing to make sure your ideas are clear and to correct any grammatical errors you have made. Your editing process can be more effective if you keep a notebook or an editing log of your common errors.

When you get a paper back from an instructor, record in your notebook any errors your instructor marked. You might also record any grammatical points that you looked up as you were writing or editing. Your log might be a single chart or checklist, as in sample 1 on page E-22. Or it might consist of sentences with errors and the corrections you make to them, as in sample 2.

When you write a new paper, check your editing log during the final stage to help you find and correct your typical mistakes.

E2-h Target specific areas for improvement.

As you master academic English, you will draw on four main skills—reading, writing, speaking, and listening—and you will develop those skills at different rates. At this point, for example, you may have more control over spoken English than over formal grammar, or you

RESOURCES See the following section of your handbook's companion Web site:
> Multilingual/ESL > Strategies for improving your academic English

SAMPLE EDITING LOG 1: CHECKLIST

Editing log (8/10-12/10)

Issues	Paper 1	Paper 2	Paper 3	Paper 4	Paper 5
Subject-verb agreement	✓✓✓	✓✓✓	✓	✓	
Verb tense	Past ✓✓✓ Future ✓✓	Past ✓✓			Past ✓
Verb form	Be + -ing form ✓✓✓	Be + -ing form ✓			
Passive voice	✓✓	✓✓	✓	✓	✓
Comma splice	✓✓✓✓	✓✓			
Fragment	✓				
Missing article	✓✓✓✓✓✓	✓✓✓✓✓	✓✓✓✓	✓✓✓	✓✓
Wrong article	✓✓✓✓	✓✓	✓✓	✓	
Missing plural form	✓✓✓✓✓	✓✓✓	✓✓✓	✓✓	✓

SAMPLE EDITING LOG 2: CORRECTED SENTENCES

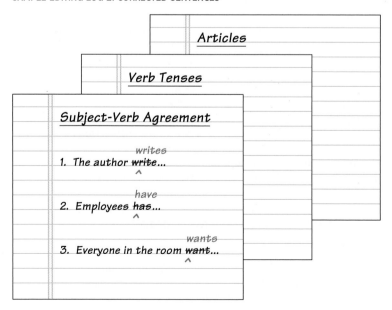

Articles

Verb Tenses

Subject-Verb Agreement

1. The author ~~write~~ writes...

2. Employees ~~has~~ have...

3. Everyone in the room ~~want~~ wants...

may have stronger reading skills than listening skills. To increase your chances of success in college, strive to balance your skills so that you can rely on strengths in not just one or two but all four skill areas.

An instructor or adviser can help you identify areas for improvement and develop strategies for building your skills.

E3 Academic writing and cultural expectations

As you challenge yourself to grow as an academic writer, pay particular attention to your readers' expectations. Some researchers have called English a "writer-responsible" language: Writers (particularly in academic and business settings) are responsible for taking a position on an issue, stating a debatable thesis, and making their ideas clear. Other languages are "reader-responsible": Writers show many sides to an issue but leave the interpretation entirely to readers.

If you are accustomed to a "reader-responsible" culture, you might find English writing surprisingly direct and assertive. Keep in mind, however, that academic readers in the United States will expect you to make a clear point and to convince them with evidence and examples that your ideas are valuable and worthy of their consideration.

E3-a In most academic papers, assert your claim before providing the evidence.

Readers in most academic situations will expect to see your claim—your thesis or main idea—before seeing your evidence or support for the claim (see "introduction" and "thesis" in your handbook). This is quite different from academic styles in some other languages, which leave the main point open to readers' interpretations or which conclude rather than begin the essay with the main idea.

If you're not accustomed to stating a thesis before providing support, you might find it useful to outline your essays carefully before beginning to write. (See "outlines" in your handbook for details on outlining.) Consider using the following steps until you feel comfortable with the academic English style:

1. Outline your ideas in the method with which you are familiar (for example, with the main idea or claim at the end).
2. Read your outline and highlight the main idea and the supporting points in your outline.

3. Rearrange your outline so that the main idea is at the beginning.
4. Use your rearranged outline as a guide when you draft your essay.

Don't be concerned if this planning stage takes time. Remember that the planning stage of writing often takes longer than the writing stage does.

The first sample outline on this page shows several points of support, leading up to the main point in the last sentence. The revised outline shows the preferred organization for an academic English essay, with the main point stated first, followed by the evidence or support.

ORIGINAL OUTLINE: MAIN IDEA LAST

1. In the United States, teenagers often move out of their parents' homes when they turn eighteen.

2. The parents' money is considered only the parents' money—not the money of their adult children.

3. Without their parents' financial help, young adults in the United States often struggle to find affordable housing, transportation, and jobs to pay for all their needs.

4. The fast pace of their daily activities and their lack of job security can be very stressful.

5. Even after they finish school, young adults in the United States may need their parents' support to achieve lasting independence.

REVISED OUTLINE: MAIN IDEA FIRST

1. Even after they finish school, young adults in the United States may need their parents' support to achieve lasting independence.

2. In the United States, teenagers move out of their parents' homes when they turn eighteen.

3. The parents' money is considered only the parents' money—not the money of their adult children.

4. Without their parents' financial help, young adults in the United States often struggle to find affordable housing, transportation, and jobs to pay for all their needs.

5. The fast pace of their daily activities and their lack of job security can be very stressful.

NOTE: In most cases, each paragraph should state a main point first, followed by supporting evidence (see "evidence" in your handbook).

There are, however, some exceptions to this pattern, particularly in the introductory and concluding paragraphs of an essay (see "paragraphs" in your handbook).

E3-b Take a stand on an issue.

As an academic writer, you will need to take a stand, to convince readers of your position in a debate. Although you must present opposing views fairly, you should clearly state your own position and the evidence to support that position. Your readers will expect you to take one side and to argue reasonably that your position is better or stronger than other positions. (See "constructing arguments" in your handbook.) Here is an example of a paragraph that was revised to stay focused on one side of an issue.

ORIGINAL: DOES NOT TAKE A STAND

Most experts in the United States agree that spanking is not an appropriate form of discipline for children. Some people, however, feel that spanking is acceptable because it can correct rude behavior. Spanking may lead to larger problems of fear and anxiety. Many children experience no lasting emotional problems from it. Opinions differ on this controversial topic.

REVISED: TAKES A STAND

Most experts in the United States agree that spanking is not an appropriate form of discipline for children. Spanking may temporarily correct rude behavior, but it may lead to larger problems such as increased aggression, and it may teach children that violence is an acceptable means of getting what they want ("Guidance" 726). Spanking should be used sparingly as a discipline option.

The original version does not take a stand on the issue of spanking. It only points out that there are differing views on the subject. In the revision, the writer takes a position and uses expert opinion (an article from the journal of the American Academy of Pediatrics) for support. (For advice about using sources in your paper, see "citing sources" in your handbook.)

E3-c Include details that support the main idea directly.

In most cases, academic readers in the United States expect writing to stay focused, each sentence supporting the main point of its paragraph. Your writing should include details, of course, but each detail should directly support your main point. Otherwise readers may think that you have lost your focus or are wasting their time.

If you like to include long descriptions or details that are interesting but not *directly* related to the main idea, or if this style is valued in your home culture, you might need to change your style to suit your new college audience. To recognize what academic English readers consider necessary details, try reading student papers that are considered effective models of academic writing. Often the best way to improve your own writing skills is to review several models.

In the following paragraph, the writer wanders off the topic (see the highlighted sentence). In the revision, each detail supports the main idea of the paragraph, and there are no unnecessary details.

PARAGRAPH WITH UNNECESSARY DETAILS

The gray wolf may not be as harmful to cattle ranching as some believe. Many residents of the western United States are opposed to allowing the gray wolf into western wilderness areas because they believe that the wolves will kill ranchers' herds and ruin their businesses. However, in the last few years, very few cows have been killed by wolves, while thousands of cows have been killed by lightning, storms, and other animals, including coyotes. Although the coyote is related to the wolf and inhabits the same areas, it is lighter in color and smaller in size. While wolves may cause some economic losses, to say that wolves alone will ruin the ranching business overstates the animals' actual impact.

FOCUSED PARAGRAPH

The gray wolf may not be as harmful to cattle ranching as some believe. Many residents of the western United States are opposed to allowing the gray wolf into western wilderness areas because they believe that the wolves will kill ranchers' herds and ruin their businesses. However, in the last few years, very few cows have been killed by wolves, while thousands of cows have been killed by lightning, storms, and other animals, including coyotes. While wolves may cause some economic losses, to say that wolves alone will ruin the ranching business overstates the animals' actual impact.

E3-d Learn to recognize intellectual property and avoid accidental plagiarism.

In some cultures, memorizing or copying exact words from texts without mentioning the authors of those sources is acceptable and

MODELS See the following section of your handbook's companion Web site:
> Model papers

sometimes encouraged. In the United States, however, the exact language, images, and original ideas contained in any published work are considered *intellectual property*, which is legally protected as if it were physical property.

When you write papers for your college classes, your instructors will expect you to give credit whenever you include an author's intellectual property in your own paper. You credit the author by citing your sources (see "citing sources" in your handbook). If you do not properly cite your sources, you might unintentionally commit a form of academic dishonesty called *plagiarism*. Most colleges in the United States take plagiarism very seriously: If a student plagiarizes, even accidentally, the student might fail the assignment or the course.

Recognizing intellectual property

Knowing what is and isn't intellectual property can be difficult. When you are writing a research paper or any essay that includes ideas from other authors, you can use the chart on pages E-28 and E-29 to help you determine whether those ideas are someone else's intellectual property. If you need additional help, review a draft of your paper with your instructor or a tutor at your school's writing center. It is important that you catch any accidental plagiarism before you turn in your work.

Avoiding plagiarism by integrating and citing sources

When you use other writers' ideas in your paper, you must follow standard academic conventions for citing, or giving credit to, the authors—a practice called *integrating sources*. There are three methods for integrating sources in your paper: summarizing, paraphrasing, and quoting (see pp. E-30 to E-32). At times, you might combine these methods to present an author's ideas.

The chart on pages E-30 to E-32 shows how to summarize, paraphrase, and quote from a source. For more on writing with sources, see "integrating sources" and "citing sources" in your handbook. Remember that whenever you summarize, paraphrase, or quote other sources in your paper, you must also provide a list of those sources at the end of your paper. This list is called Works Cited in MLA style, References in APA style, and Bibliography in *Chicago* (CMS) style. For details, see "documenting sources" in your handbook.

Recognizing intellectual property

Intellectual property

The first column shows the types of information that are considered intellectual property. The second column gives examples from student essays that use and cite sources with the MLA style of documentation (used in English and some humanities). See the MLA section of your handbook for complete details about citing sources in your paper and in the list of works cited in MLA style. See the APA section or the *Chicago* (CMS) section of your handbook if your instructor or discipline requires one of those styles instead.

Type of information	Examples with appropriate citations
Any *exact* words from a published source (even if the source provides a fact)	**IN-TEXT CITATION** Luis N. Rivera writes, "Five hundred years ago, thanks to the nautical audacity and cosmographical ignorance of an Italian mariner . . . the Atlantic Ocean ceased to be a divider and became the waterway connection between Europe, Africa, and the Americas" (270). **WORKS CITED ENTRY** Rivera, Luis N. *A Violent Evangelism*. Louisville: Westminster, 1992. Print.
Any original ideas from a published source—even if you've paraphrased the source (written the information in your own words)	**IN-TEXT CITATION** Historian Paul Gordon Lauren shows that even though the First World War did not seem to be about race at first, a number of racial issues had surfaced by the time the war ended in 1918 (75). **WORKS CITED ENTRY** Lauren, Paul Gordon. *Power and Prejudice*. 2nd ed. Boulder: Westview, 1996. Print.
Results of a study	**IN-TEXT CITATION** One study showed that cutting down trees that have been burned in forest fires prevents new trees from growing in the area (Donato et al. 352). **WORKS CITED ENTRY** Donato, D. C., et al. "Post-Wildfire Logging Hinders Regeneration and Increases Fire Risk." *Science* 311.5759 (2006): 352. Print.
Statistics	**IN-TEXT CITATION** Gore writes, "In 1988, the EPA reported that the ground water in thirty-two states was

Type of information	Examples with appropriate citations
	contaminated with seventy-four different agricultural chemicals, including one, herbicide atrazine, that is classified as a potential human carcinogen" (xxii-xxiii).
	WORKS CITED ENTRY Gore, Al. Introduction. *Silent Spring*. By Rachel Carson. Boston: Houghton, 1994. xv-xxvi. Print.
Theories	**IN-TEXT CITATION** While many linguists have argued that language is a "cultural invention," Steven Pinker claims that language is an "instinct"; he writes that it is "not a cultural artifact" but "a distinct piece of the biological makeup of our brains" (4).
	WORKS CITED ENTRY Pinker, Stephen. *The Language Instinct*. New York: Perennial, 2000. Print.

Not intellectual property

The first column shows the types of information that are *not* considered intellectual property and that may be used in a paper without citing a source. The second column gives examples of each type.

Type of information	Examples
Well-known historical, scientific, or cultural facts	Christopher Columbus sailed across the Atlantic Ocean in 1492. World War I ended in 1918. Forest fires are sometimes caused by lightning. Rachel Carson wrote *Silent Spring*.
Broad, general observations	Many languages are spoken in the United States. Some students tend to have more motivation than others. Many US residents own cars and computers.

NOTE: For types of information not on this list, check with your instructor or your school's writing center to determine whether you need to cite the source. When in doubt, cite the source.

Integrating and citing sources
Summarizing, paraphrasing, quoting, and documenting

The following annotated source passages and sample summary, paraphrase, quotation, and MLA-style citation show how one student thought about and integrated a source into a paper for an introduction to psychology course.

Summarizing

When you summarize a source, you express another author's ideas in your own words, using fewer words than the author used. Even though a summary is in your own words, the original idea remains the intellectual property of the author, so you must include a citation.

To summarize effectively, try annotating the source text to identify the focus of the passage. Then, using your own words, present the main idea or ideas, leaving out detailed illustrations and examples.

ORIGINAL SOURCE PASSAGE (WEBBER, "MAKE YOUR OWN LUCK," 65)

Serendipity = luck.

Ignore the surgeon example—too much detail.

Serendipity smiles upon people who have a more relaxed approach to life. They have clarified their long-term goals but don't worry too much about the details. Rather than aiming to become the top cardiac surgeon at the Mayo Clinic, they vow to be a doctor who helps save lives. Once they've pinpointed the ultimate destination, they believe there are many different ways to get there. This requires openness to life's surprising twists and turns as well as cognitive and behavioral flexibility.

Main idea = Lucky people are adaptable and open to new possibilities.

The signal phrase credits the author and introduces the summary.

SUMMARY

Webber reports that lucky people tend to be adaptable; in other words, luck comes to those who are open to new possibilities (65).

The summary conveys only the main idea of the source passage.

The page number shows where the summary ends and where this idea can be found in the source.

Paraphrasing

When you paraphrase, you express an author's idea in your own words, using approximately the same number of words as in the source. Even though the words are your own, the original idea is the author's intellectual property, so you must give a citation.

ORIGINAL SOURCE PASSAGE (WEBBER, "MAKE YOUR OWN LUCK," 66)

take in more visual information, while those in bad moods don't see as much around them.

Focus on fear = loss of opportunity.

Anxiety in particular gives us tunnel vision; while we're focusing on a potential danger, we end up missing a lot of extraneous but potentially beneficial information. In another experiment, people were offered a large financial reward to carefully watch a dot on a computer screen. Occasional

INEFFECTIVE PARAPHRASE (PLAGIARIZED)

According to Webber, anxiety gives us a narrow view; when we're focusing on something dangerous, we might not notice potentially helpful information that is also available (66).

Because the sentence structure and phrasing are too similar to those of the original, the attempted paraphrase is plagiarized. This student has merely replaced a few of the author's words with synonyms. *Gives us a narrow view* is too similar to *gives us tunnel vision. Potentially helpful information* is almost the same as *potentially beneficial information.*

To paraphrase effectively, be sure that you thoroughly understand the source text. After you have read the passage you want to paraphrase, set the source aside. State in your own words the author's key ideas. Then look at the source again to be sure that you haven't used the author's exact words or sentence structure.

EFFECTIVE PARAPHRASE

The signal phrase credits the author and shows where the paraphrase begins.

Webber points out that people might miss out on lucky opportunities if they are nervous. Their nervousness causes them to block out extra information that could help them in some way (66).

The page number shows where the paraphrase ends and where this idea appears in the source text.

The revised paraphrase conveys the author's original idea but uses the student's voice. No phrases are plagiarized.

Quoting

When you quote a source, you copy some of the author's exact words and enclose them in quotation marks. Quotation marks show your readers that both the idea and the words belong to the author.

To quote effectively, give your readers enough information to understand how the quotation relates to your own ideas. Introduce the quotation in your own words and then explain it so that your readers understand its significance.

ORIGINAL SOURCE PASSAGE (WEBBER, "MAKE YOUR OWN LUCK," 67)

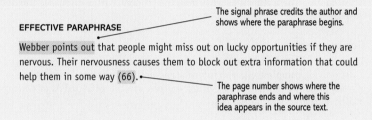

Serendipitous people are more fearless about trying something new. Instead of giving in to worry about what could go wrong, they think, "Isn't that interesting? I'd like to give that a try."

Good outcomes increase self-efficacy, or the belief that you are capable of accomplishing whatever you set out to do; they also fuel an appetite for future risk.

Lucky people aren't afraid to take risks.

"Fuel an appetite for future risk" = make people want to take more risks.

The signal phrase credits the author and shows where the cited information begins.

The transition (*In fact*) and the signal phrase (*she writes*) link the quotation to the rest of the student's discussion.

EFFECTIVE QUOTATION

Webber explains that lucky people aren't afraid to take risks. In fact, she writes that the "good outcomes" of taking risks "increase self-efficacy, or the belief that you are capable of accomplishing whatever you set out to do; they also fuel an appetite for future risk" (67). Those who think of themselves as lucky have simply decided to focus on the positive results of risk taking, instead of worrying about the risk of failure.

The page number shows where the cited information ends and where the passage appears in the source text.

The author's exact words appear inside quotation marks.

After quoting the author's exact words, the student writer discusses the quotation.

Documenting

To give proper credit to any sources you summarize, paraphrase, or quote, you must provide complete citation information on the works cited page at the end of your paper. (For more about citing sources, see the MLA, APA, or *Chicago* [CMS] section in your handbook.)

SAMPLE ENTRY IN AN MLA WORKS CITED LIST

Webber, Rebecca. "Make Your Own Luck." *Psychology Today* June 2010: 62-68. Print.

E3-e Sample student essay

The following brief argument paper was written by Amy Zhang, a student in a composition class. The first version (pp. E-33 to E-35) shows Zhang's initial draft with her instructor's comments. The second version (pp. E-36 to E-39) is Zhang's final draft.

ROUGH DRAFT, WITH INSTRUCTOR'S COMMENTS

Zhang 1

Amy Zhang

Professor Swain

English 101

16 October 2008

The Importance of Food

The title needs to be more focused. A clearer thesis in the first paragraph may help.

If you drive on any highway in the United States, you will see many fast-food restaurant. Most supermarkets are full of prepared foods that say "make it in minutes" and "ready to serve." According to article by James Bone on *TimesOnline* Web site, only one-third of Americans cook meals from scratch. Bone also write that Americans spend only thirty minutes cooking dinner, but they spent 2 ½ hours in the 1960s. In his book *Fast Food Nation*, Eric Schlosser says that one-quarter of Americans eat in a fast-food restaurant each day (3).

Missing articles

Verb form

Missing article with proper noun

The opening paragraph needs a clear thesis.

In most families in United States, two people are working (Bone), and people with full-time jobs don't have time for food shopping and cooking meals. Instead of coming home from work at night and cooking, many people prefer to heat something in their microwave or get takeout from a restaurant. This is why Americans are eating fast food so often—they don't have enough time. *Try moving it to the beginning of the paragraph.*

Is this the main point of the paragraph?

And even if Americans did have more time to cook every night, it is hard for them to find good fresh food. Supermarkets have many foods in cans and boxes, but they sometimes don't have much fresh meat and vegetables.

This paragraph strays from the main topic of the paper. Consider deleting it.

Another reason that mealtime has become so short is that many younger adults grew up eating fast food for almost all meals. In the past fifteen years, cell phones, the Internet, and e-mail have increased the speed of everyday communication. At the same time, microwave oven, drive-through restaurant, and frozen dinner have changed the way Americans eat. Many people now like to eat quickly, even in their cars or in front of the television, instead of take time to cook a meal and sit at the table. When people are used to everything fast in their lives, they don't think food is important enough to spend much time on.

Use plural nouns for general categories.

Noun ("-ing" form) after preposition

Americans' obsession with fast food has caused the quality of their lives to go down. First of all, their health is suffering. As most people

Zhang 2

Missing linking verb

know, fast foods and frozen meals generally less healthy than foods made at home. They have lots of preservatives, fat, sugar, and salt to hide the

No "will" in "if" clause

fact that they are not fresh. If people will not eat fresh foods that provide vitamins and minerals, they may become tired and sick, and they may miss out on opportunities to enjoy their lives.

Place-holder "There" missing

Possible plagiarism. Check the source. If the words are directly from the source, use quotation marks.

Another serious health problem is obesity. Is an obesity epidemic in the United States today, especially with young people, and it's related to the way people are eating. According to Schlosser, "The rate of obesity among American children is twice as high as it was in the late 1970s" (240). Obesity can lead to many health problems, including diabetes, heart disease, and cancer. The United States Department of Health and Human Services notes that deaths due to poor diet and physical inactivity increased 33 percent in the 1990s and may soon overtake tobacco as the leading cause of death in the United States. If fast food causes people to become obese, and then obesity causes them to get sick or die, fast food

Passive verb form

cannot be consider an "improvement" in Americans' lives.

The economy causes most people to work long hours, so they don't have time for cooking and they rely on fast food. It makes life much easier

This paragraph may confuse

and allows parents to get other things done around the house and spend time with their children. If they try hard enough, people can even find healthy options at fast-food restaurants, such as salads and bottled water instead of fries and sodas. So maybe fast food isn't always a bad thing.

readers—it takes the opposite view of your main point. Revise it to acknowledge the opposing view without contradicting your main point.

The end of the essay needs development. Readers expect a strong ending with a clear point, not an open-ended statement.

Zhang 3

Works Cited

Bone, James. "Good Home Cooking—Right off the Assembly Line."
  TimesOnline 27 Mar. 2006. Web. 9 Oct. 2008.

Schlosser, Eric. *Fast Food Nation: The Dark Side of the All-American Meal.*
  Boston: Houghton, 2001. Print.

United States. Dept. of Health and Human Services. "Citing 'Dangerous
  Increase' in Deaths, HHS Launches New Strategies against Overweight
  Epidemic." *HHS.gov.* 10 Mar. 2004. Web. 9 Oct. 2008.

For an online source, give the sponsor.

FINAL DRAFT

Zhang 1

Amy Zhang

Professor Swain

English 101

23 October 2008

Slow Down and Eat Better

Zhang opens with general observations to attract readers' interest.

> If you drive on any highway in the United States, you'll find fast-food restaurants at every exit and service area. If you walk through any supermarket, you'll see prepared foods that say "make it in minutes" and "ready to serve." According to an article by James Bone on the *TimesOnline* Web site, only one-third of Americans cook meals from scratch, meaning with fresh ingredients. Bone also writes that Americans spend only thirty minutes cooking dinner, compared with 2½ hours in the 1960s. And in his book *Fast Food Nation*, Eric Schlosser claims that one-quarter of Americans eat in a fast-food restaurant each day (3). Why are Americans eating so much fast food? The answer is simple: speed is more important than quality. While Americans may be attracted to food that is fast and easy,

Zhang states a clear thesis at the end of the opening paragraph.

> they are missing the benefits of slowing down. In fact, Americans' obsession with fast food is hurting not only their health but also the quality of their lives.

> The main reason that Americans are getting takeout food and heating prepared meals is obvious: they don't have enough time. In more than two-thirds of families in the United States, two people are working (Bone). People with demanding work schedules have no time for food shopping and cooking.

A clear topic sentence helps guide readers.

> Another reason that mealtime has become so short is that many younger adults grew up in a fast-food culture. In the past fifteen years, cell phones, the Internet, and e-mail have increased the speed of everyday communication. At the same time, microwave ovens, drive-through restaurants, and frozen dinners have changed the way Americans eat. Many people now like to eat quickly, even in their cars or in front of the television, instead of taking time to cook a meal and sit at the table. In this culture of instant gratification, people don't think food is important enough to spend much time on.

A transition links the ideas in this paragraph and in the previous paragraph.

> Even though Americans think that they are saving time and improving their lives by eating precooked and prepackaged food, their

---

Marginal annotations indicate MLA-style formatting and effective writing.

obsession with fast food is causing the quality of their lives to go down. First, their health is suffering. As most people know, fast foods and frozen meals are generally less healthy than foods made at home. They have lots of preservatives, fat, sugar, and salt to hide the fact that they are not fresh. If people do not eat fresh foods that provide vitamins and minerals, they may become tired and sick, and they may miss out on opportunities to enjoy their lives.

Another serious health problem is obesity. There is an obesity epidemic in the United States today, especially with young people, and it is related to the way people are eating. According to Schlosser, "The rate of obesity among American children is twice as high as it was in the late 1970s" (240). Obesity can lead to many health problems, including diabetes, heart disease, and cancer. The United States Department of Health and Human Services notes that "deaths due to poor diet and physical inactivity increased 33 percent" in the 1990s, and it cites a study that concluded that "poor diet and physical inactivity may soon overtake tobacco as the leading cause of death" in the United States. If fast food causes people to become obese, and then obesity causes them to get sick or die, fast food cannot be considered an "improvement" in Americans' lives.

In addition to causing health problems, fast food hurts people's relationships with their friends and families. In an online interview, John Robbins, author of *Diet for a New America* and *The Food Revolution*, comments on the importance of mealtime:

> Throughout history, eating has been a way of bringing people together. It's how parents stay in touch with what's going on in their kids' lives. When people break bread together, it's an act of peacemaking, an act of good will. . . . Dining together can be a deep biological and sacred experience. When we eat, we are connected to all of life. It's a phenomenon found in every culture in the world, except ours. I see the McDonaldization of our food supply as the annihilation of our true relationship to life. (qtd. in Lee)

While most Americans will not be able to cook full, fresh meals every day, they can begin to improve the quality of their lives by buying fresh foods when they can and by cooking fresh food at least sometimes. For

---

Marginal annotations:

Zhang uses a signal phrase and a parenthetical citation for facts that support her thesis.

No page number is available for this online source.

A long quotation (more than four lines) is indented; quotation marks are omitted. An ellipsis mark indicates that some words from the source have been left out.

Zhang acknowledges the limitations of her argument while maintaining her position.

Zhang offers readers some suggestions for better eating.

example, people can shop at the farmers' market for fresh local produce instead of buying canned or frozen vegetables. They will have a chance to buy foods with more nutrients at the same time that they get to know people in their community.

Also, if people slow down to make food with their friends or family, they can enjoy the benefits of good nutrition while they are building stronger relationships. An organization called Slow Food, which describes itself as "an international organization whose aim is to protect the pleasures of the table from the homogenization of modern fast food and life," encourages readers of its Web site to make pasta from scratch once in a while. Friends and family can cook meals together so one person isn't doing all the work. And people can try to cook family recipes from their parents or grandparents.

The conclusion reminds readers of the essay's main point.

Even though Americans may think they are saving time and improving their lives by eating fast food, they will actually have healthier and more enjoyable lives if they change the way they cook and eat. Making dinner from scratch is much healthier than getting burgers and fries from a fast-food restaurant. And people get more than just a full stomach—they get more time with family and friends and a good feeling from creating something healthy.

Zhang 4

Works Cited

Bone, James. "Good Home Cooking—Right off the Assembly Line." *TimesOnline*. Times Newspapers, 27 Mar. 2006. Web. 9 Oct. 2008.

Lee, Virginia. "The *Common Ground* Interview with John Robbins." *The Food Revolution*. John Robbins, 2002. Web. 18 Oct. 2008.

Schlosser, Eric. *Fast Food Nation: The Dark Side of the All-American Meal*. Boston: Houghton, 2002. Print.

Slow Food. *Slowfood.com*. Slow Food, n.d. Web. 18 Oct. 2008.

United States. Dept. of Health and Human Services. "Citing 'Dangerous Increase' in Deaths, HHS Launches New Strategies against Overweight Epidemic." *HHS.gov*. US Dept. of Health and Human Services, 10 Mar. 2004. Web. 9 Oct. 2008.

The works cited list provides references for all the sources Zhang uses in her paper.

≡ **E4** Practice exercises

This section includes both intensive and extensive grammar and writing exercises. The intensive activities will help you focus on specific areas of grammar such as verb tense and use of articles. The extensive activities will help build your English fluency—your ability to use English quickly and easily without hesitating or translating from your native language.

E4-a Intensive grammar exercises

The intensive exercises in this section can help you improve your awareness and proper use of the English grammar covered in the grammar sections of your handbook. These exercises will also help you strengthen your editing skills when you edit your own writing in English. (For help building fluency rather than grammar and editing skills, see the extensive writing practices in E4-b, starting on p. E-49.) Answers to all the exercises appear at the end of this section.

EXERCISE E1–1 Verb forms and tenses   Edit the following sentences to correct errors in verb forms and verb tenses. If a sentence is correct, write "correct" after it. (For help, see "verb form and tense" in the multilingual/ESL section of your handbook. You may need to refer to the chart on irregular verbs as well.) Example:

> *moved*
> I ~~move~~ to Florida three years ago.
> ^

1. When she got home, Mina realize that she had forgotten to buy staples while she was out.
2. Martin Luther King Jr., the famous orator and civil rights activist, deliver his famous "I Have a Dream" speech on August 28, 1963.
3. David was playing soccer for the last fifteen years.
4. Mangoes, which originally grew only in Asia, now grew in the Eastern and Western Hemispheres.
5. Anders has already read *To Kill a Mockingbird* three times.
6. Alexander Fleming discovered penicillin while he was worked at a hospital in London.
7. Moving to a new country often cause people to change their lifestyles.
8. Although anthropologists do not know exactly when the first calendar was invented, they have evidence that solar calendars are existing for at least six thousand years.

9. When they moved here, my husband and his brother open a small restaurant.
10. Professors in the United States often requiring their students to work in groups.

EXERCISE E1–2 Verb forms and tenses Edit the following sentences to correct errors in verb forms and verb tenses. If a sentence is correct, write "correct" after it. (For help, see "verb form and tense" in the multilingual/ESL section of your handbook. You may need to refer to the chart on irregular verbs as well.) Example:

loved
Amy ~~was loving~~ Woody Guthrie's songs when she was a child.
^

1. Woody Guthrie was being one of the best-known American folk singer–activists.
2. Born in 1912, Guthrie spend his early life surrounded by music in his small hometown of Okema, Oklahoma.
3. Before his twentieth birthday, he was moving to Texas, where he attempted to start a career as a musician.
4. While Guthrie was in Texas, a decade-long period of dust storms began sweeping through the central United States.
5. Guthrie and his family move west to California along with many other Texans and Oklahomans who found employment as farmworkers.
6. While he was traveled, he was exposed to the harsh treatment the migrant workers received.
7. By the time Guthrie arrive in California, he had developed a deep sense of resentment for the rich owners who exploited poor farmworkers.
8. He begin writing and singing more songs about workers' rights and political protest, including his most famous song, "This Land Is Your Land."
9. He continued writing songs with a political message for the rest of his life and motivate many other popular folk and rock singers to carry on his legacy.
10. Today, Guthrie's music live on in younger generations of people who feel inspired by his words.

EXERCISE E1–3 Verb forms and tenses Edit the following paragraph to correct errors in verb forms and verb tenses. There are ten errors. (For help, see "verb form and tense" in the multilingual/ESL section of your handbook. You may need to refer to the chart on irregular verbs as well.)

When Julie had visited the museum yesterday, she learn about the life cycle of the butterfly. The scientist at the museum explain the typical process: A butterfly, like all other insects, is beginning its life as an egg. When the egg hatches, a caterpillar emerge. The caterpillar spend its short life eating leaves on its host plant, growing larger in preparation for its transformation. After about two weeks, the caterpillar attaches itself to a stem and forms a chrysalis, a type of shell that protected it while it changes into a butterfly. After it is finish growing inside the chrysalis, the butterfly emerges. It rests on a leaf or stem while its wings dried and become stronger. When its wings become strong enough, it fly away.

EXERCISE E1–4 Modal verbs   In the following dialogue, choose the correct modal verb or verb phrase in parentheses. (For help, see "modal verbs" in the multilingual/ESL section of your handbook.)

> HALEY: Good morning, Professor Weil. (May / Would) I ask you for some advice about my course work?
>
> PROFESSOR WEIL: Sure, Haley. What (can / will) I help you with?
>
> H: I (will / would) like to change my major. I'm enrolled as a biology major now, but I am not as interested in science as I thought I (will be / would be).
>
> P: I see. What major are you thinking of?
>
> H: Since I am very good at math, I think I would like to be a business major.
>
> P: That's a good idea, but (can / may) you do well in classes that don't involve math?
>
> H: I think so. Which courses (must I to take / must I take) besides math?
>
> P: You will have to take some communications and writing courses.
>
> H: I (can do / can to do) that. I will go to the registrar and select my courses. Thank you, Professor Weil!

EXERCISE E1–5 Passive verb forms   Edit the following paragraph to correct errors in passive verb forms. There are ten errors. (For help, see "verb form and tense" in the multilingual/ESL section of your handbook. You may need to refer to the chart on irregular verbs as well.)

> Most people think of a trash bin as a finishing point rather than a starting point. However, a recycling bin can be the start of a new life for a piece of paper. After paper is put into an office bin, it is ship to a recycling center, where it is sorting into types: office paper, cardboard, or colored paper. After it is sorted, it is sended to a paper mill, where it is chop into dry pulp. The pulp is then mixed with water to form a wet substance called "slurry." The slurry is sent through a screen, which removes little bits of excess materials such as glue, plastic, or staples.

After it goes through the screen, the slurry is rinse again to remove inks. Then the slurry goes through a machine that makes the paper fibers grow bigger. Next the slurry is water down and place on a screen, where it is press into long, thin sheets and dried on heated rollers. The dried sheets are rolling up and shipped off to other companies where they are process and made into the paper products we use every day.

EXERCISE E1–6 Negative verb forms Edit the following sentences to correct errors in the use of negative verb forms. (For help, see "negative verb forms" in the multilingual/ESL section of your handbook.) Example:

> *not*
> Even though I was tired, I could ~~no~~ sleep.
>   ^

1. If the governor is reelected, she not will raise the income tax.
2. I could no park my car next to the library because all of the spaces were taken.
3. Sadly, a cure for AIDS has no been found yet.
4. The book that we have to buy for our ecology class not is very expensive.
5. I tried to make a photocopy, but the copier was no functioning properly.
6. Sunnie did not came with us to the football game last Saturday.
7. Although Omar not like to drive in traffic, he likes to race cars on the weekends.
8. Snow leopards no are extinct, but they are on the endangered species list.
9. Kim could not find no lychees at the supermarket because they are not very common in the United States.
10. I was disappointed that I didn't knew the woman's name.

EXERCISE E1–7 Conditional sentences Edit the following conditional sentences to correct any problems with verbs. If a sentence is correct, write "correct" after it. (For help, see "conditional verbs" in the multilingual/ESL section of your handbook.) Example:

> If the Chargers ~~will~~ win the game tonight, they will move on to the
>
> district finals.

1. If Deborah arrived earlier, she might have found a better parking space.
2. I'll buy you a soda if you will come to the cafeteria with me.
3. The city will not increase the sales tax unless the citizens vote in favor of the new tax law.
4. Most scientists think that if the world does not reduce carbon dioxide emissions, global warming will occur.
5. If I was a famous actor, I would move to Bel Aire and buy a mansion.

6. If you will use aloe on a burn, you can reduce the chances of developing a scar.
7. You would have to pay late charges if you don't return your movie rental on time.
8. Unless the Security Council will agree, the UN will not send peacekeeping troops to war-torn countries.
9. When Rosa left for college every September, she closes her summer gardening business.
10. If Kevin would be here with us today, he would be enjoying himself.

EXERCISE E1–8 Verbs followed by gerunds or infinitives Edit the following paragraph to correct problems with verbs followed by gerunds or infinitives. There are eight errors. (For help, see "verbs followed by gerunds or infinitives" in the multilingual/ESL section of your handbook.)

When I was young, my family and I went on an annual camping trip in the canyons of the southwestern United States. One summer, I convinced my family taking a tour of several canyons: the Grand Canyon, Bryce Canyon, and Canyonlands National Park. I remember to be amazed at each stop along the way. I loved looking up at the twisting towers of red rock, wondering how they had avoided to fall down in the last several thousand years. (I can recall to think that some might fall over if someone in the canyon sneezed a little too hard.) Even at that young age, I sensed the power of these remarkable landmarks and understood the spell that they had held over so many generations of residents and visitors. In my heart, I promised going back to the canyons every year. Though I never planned giving up my promise, the commitments of adulthood have prevented me from taking annual trips back to the canyons. I miss to visit the red rocks on a regular basis, but I still manage going back to the Southwest every few years. Breathing in the high desert air while gazing up at the red rock towers never ceases to refresh and rejuvenate me.

EXERCISE E2–1 Linking verbs Add linking verbs where necessary in the following paragraphs. There are seven missing verbs. (For help, see "linking verbs" in the multilingual/ESL section of your handbook.)

When I a child, I did not like to work. Every time my parents asked me to clean my room or study for my classes, I always found an excuse. Sometimes I would pretend that I too tired; other times I would pretend that I had simply forgotten their request. Most of the time, however, I would try to approach the situation logically, arguing that since my older brother stronger and had more life experience, he should be responsible for most of the household chores.

However, when I started college, my life changed. I realized that to become the successful college student I wanted to be, I would have to take control of my life, change my bad habits, and act responsibly. Now I no longer the boy my parents knew when I was a child. I wake up early, exercise, and go to school. I never late to my classes, and I always turn my assignments in on time. Although I still far from perfect, I try to help others whenever I can. Whenever someone needs me, particularly at school or at home, I never try to hide as I did when I just a boy.

EXERCISE E2–2 Missing subjects Five sentences in the following paragraph are missing subjects. Add subjects where they are needed. (For help, see "subject in every sentence" in the multilingual/ESL section of your handbook.)

Is common to think that being the oldest child in a family has the most privileges. However, are several advantages to being the youngest child, too. First, is important to note that by the time the youngest child is born, the parents have already had experience as parents. They know how to care for a newborn, and they tend to be more relaxed. Second, the youngest child has the opportunity to learn how to stay out of trouble. If the older children get into trouble, is easy for the youngest child to learn from the older children's mistakes. A third advantage of being the youngest child is that in many cases, the youngest gets extra attention from the older siblings. Is not unusual to see older siblings taking care of their younger siblings at school or protecting them from bullies.

EXERCISE E2–3 Unnecessary words Edit the following sentences by deleting unnecessary words. (In some cases, more than one correction is possible.) If a sentence is correct, write "correct" after it. (For help, see the sections on deleting unnecessary words in the multilingual/ESL section of your handbook.) Example:

> *the food*
> ~~The food~~ I ate ~~it~~ very quickly.
>   ^

1. Coming to the United States it changed more than my address. It changed the direction of my career.
2. My life here in Gainesville it's different from the life that I lived in Bolivia.
3. When I was in Bolivia, I was a chef.
4. I attended a culinary school, which it was the best in Bolivia, and I was offered the chance to study for a short time in the United States.
5. When I first came, I met other students who they had different majors.
6. I learned many things from my roommate, Jin, who was a business major.
7. Jin he helped me realize the importance of having business experience.
8. I learned that although I enjoyed being a chef, but I didn't want to be a chef without business knowledge.

9. I decided to stay a bit longer in the United States, where I could study international business here.
10. Someday I will combine both interests and start my own chain of specialized restaurants, which I hope to build them all over the world.

EXERCISE E2–4 Placement of adverbs   Edit the following sentences to put adverbs in their proper place. If a sentence is correct, write "correct" after it. (For help, see "placement of adverbs" in the multilingual/ESL section of your handbook.) Example:

My roommate likes to play ~~very loudly~~ the drums./ *very loudly.*
                                                    ^

1. I have never seen a player hit so hard a baseball.
2. Sue cooked very slowly the soup so that the vegetables would be tender.
3. Regular study habits can help students complete all their assignments efficiently.
4. After I finished my workout, I stretched carefully my tender muscles.
5. The professor seemed surprised that the class finished so quickly the exam.
6. After I read the user manual, I installed easily the new hard drive.
7. My mother always told me that she loved equally all her children.
8. As soon as I got the keys to my new car, I drove everywhere my friends.
9. The government found out that the company manufactured illegally the drug.
10. Although she had a difficult time in the past, this year she won very easily the gold medal in cross-country skiing.

EXERCISE E3–1 Articles   Edit the following sentences to correct errors in the use of articles (*a, an, the*). (For help, see the sections on articles in the multilingual/ESL section of your handbook.) Example:

Holly recently bought *a* new sound system for her car.
                       ^

1. When people move to new place, they definitely have to go through some changes.
2. Temperature dropped twenty degrees in a half hour yesterday.
3. Some governments help couples who have more than two children by giving them the health insurance.
4. When people are too busy, they sometimes forget to eat the dinner.
5. Students are exposed to the new experiences when they move to a new country.
6. I chose to have small family so that I could give my children sufficient attention.
7. Marco became more familiar with the nature when he studied in the rain forests of Brazil.

8. Let me give you an advice: Buy your books early.
9. A common effect of culture shock is the loneliness.
10. Because our school doesn't allow cars within the campus gates, I walk from my parking spot to place where I need to go.

EXERCISE E3–2 Articles Edit the following paragraph to correct errors in the use of articles (*a, an, the*). There are ten errors. (For help, see the sections on articles in the multilingual/ESL section of your handbook.)

Heifer International is nonprofit organization that provides the animals to poor farmers and families around world. Organization was started in 1940s by man named Dan West, relief worker who gave people food during times of crisis. West realized that he could help people even more by giving them animals that could supply food—such as the milk and cheese—for several years. He wanted to help people for the long term, and he wanted to help them have the pride in themselves. Now Heifer serves communities in more than one hundred countries around world. Its mission is to help families by providing some animals that the families can use to support themselves.

EXERCISE E3–3 Articles Edit the following sentences to correct errors in the use of articles (*a, an, the*). In some cases, more than one revision is possible. (For help, see the sections on articles in the multilingual/ESL section of your handbook.)

A greeting is the way that the person addresses or acknowledges another person when the two meet. Types of greetings vary in different countries. People in the Japan often prefer to greet nonverbally, with bow and a smile. African would likely greet fellow African with the handshake. For the Maori people of New Zealand, a most common greeting is the *hongi*, which involves rubbing noses. In Poland, kiss on each cheek is customary; but the Dutch custom is to kiss the right cheek, then the left, and then the right again. Traveler to another country would be wise to learn greetings expected by its people.

EXERCISE E4–1 Present and past participles Choose the correct participle in the parentheses in the following sentences. (For help, see "participles" in the multilingual/ESL section of your handbook.) Example:

My (tiring /(tired) old dog sleeps all day.

1. Charlie thinks I'm (confusing / confused). He says that he doesn't understand me because I talk too fast and never stop to explain my thoughts.

2. My feet still hurt from the long, (tiring / tired) walk we took yesterday.
3. Alex and her boyfriend went to see a really (boring / bored) movie last night.
4. Myrna is always busy. She's a (working / worked) mom with three kids—and she goes to college!
5. Gavin said that Professor Snyder's mythology lecture was (fascinating / fascinated).
6. Is your essay (handwriting / handwritten), or is it (typing / typed)?
7. I will be (satisfying / satisfied) if I can read at least two chapters in my chemistry text over the weekend.
8. This vase is beautiful! Is it (hand-painting / hand-painted)?
9. The commercial claims that this (cleaning / cleaned) product helps kill bacteria.
10. Señora Quiroga put two cups of (peeling / peeled) apples in the bowl.

EXERCISE E5–1 Prepositions showing time and place Edit the following sentences to correct the use of prepositions. If a sentence is correct, write "correct" after it. (For help, see "prepositions" in the multilingual/ESL section of your handbook.) Example:

> *on*
> The office will be closed ~~at~~ Memorial Day.
>   ^

1. Does your dance class start in Monday or Wednesday?
2. Fran was working at her desk when the earthquake hit.
3. As soon as Fiona moved into her dorm room, she put a poster of Einstein in the wall for inspiration.
4. My books are a little dusty because they were packed away on the garage for a year.
5. Dr. Horn is taking his students to Ghana for a study trip on early June.
6. My grandmother was born at Los Angeles, but my grandfather was born at Albuquerque.
7. My fraternity brothers like to play loud music at the street in front of our building.
8. My exam begins at two hours, but I'm not nervous at all.
9. Did you read the essay in *The Bedford Reader*, or were you able to find it on the Internet?
10. Bret finished writing his term paper right on midnight.

EXERCISE E5–2 Preposition combinations Edit the following sentences for errors in preposition combinations (preposition + noun, adjective + preposition, or verb + preposition). If a sentence is correct, write "correct" after it. (See "prepositions" in the multilingual/ESL section of your handbook.) Example:

> *about*
> Sandra has been dreaming ~~with~~ becoming a doctor.
>   ^

1. I have trouble concentrating in my homework when my roommate is around.
2. The senator was skilled at delay controversial votes.
3. I'm not worried with our verbs test on Wednesday.
4. While Ellie proofread the group's report, Sam and Tomi worked in the presentation slides.
5. The executives were found guilty of insider trading.
6. The solution consists in sodium and water.
7. I was afraid to board the plane because I'm not accustomed with traveling alone.
8. Shea remained devoted on the teachings of his martial arts master.
9. You can always count with Carole to help out when the office gets busy.
10. Iona wasn't aware of the trouble the manager was experiencing.

E4-b Topics for writing practice

The writing prompts beginning on page E-50 can help you build fluency and confidence in using English grammar in academic situations. Use the prompts in conjunction with the intensive and extensive practice instructions on this page and the next. If you would like to focus on points of grammar, sentence structure, essay development, or editing skills, use the directions for intensive practice. If you would like to develop your fluency—your ability to write in English without translating from your native language—use the directions for extensive practice. Each prompt is accompanied by a suggested writing focus, which can be used with either the intensive or the extensive practice.

Directions for intensive practice (focus on grammar and on writing and editing skills)

1. Write a paragraph or an essay on one of the prompts beginning on page E-50.
2. Edit and revise your work carefully, paying attention to the suggested writing focus (or any other focus your instructor recommends).
3. Take your finished work to your instructor or to the writing center for a conference. If you take your work to the writing center, explain to the tutor that this is a practice exercise and that you would like help with the specific area you focused on.
4. Use your editing log to record any repeated mistakes you've made so that you can be aware of them and try to eliminate them in future writing assignments. (See E2-g for advice about editing logs.)

Directions for extensive practice (focus on fluency and speed)

1. Choose one of the prompts beginning on this page and set aside a specific amount of time to write (fifteen minutes, thirty minutes, or one hour, for example). Pay special attention to the suggested writing focus in the prompt (or any other focus your instructor recommends).
2. Begin writing and try not to stop until the end of the period you have set. You might find it helpful to set an alarm or a timer.
3. When you are finished, reread your work and highlight the parts of your writing that you like best.
4. If you feel comfortable, read your work to someone else—a roommate, friend, or family member.
5. Keep your extensive writing in a folder or binder so that you can refer to it as a source of ideas for future writing assignments.

Writing prompts

1. In a paragraph or an essay, discuss the attributes of a person who has had a significant impact on history. *Suggested writing focus:* verb tenses and forms.
2. Write a paragraph or an essay about a time when you were afraid. What did you do? How did you overcome your fear? *Suggested writing focus:* verb tenses and forms.
3. Spend a few minutes reflecting on the last five years of your life. In a paragraph or an essay, describe how you have changed during this time. *Suggested writing focus:* verb tenses and forms.
4. Imagine that you could give advice to any historical figure. To whom would you give advice? What would that advice be? Write a dialogue (a conversation) in which you give this person the advice you think he or she needs. *Suggested writing focus:* modal verbs (for example, "you *could* . . . ," "you *should* . . .").
5. Write a paragraph or an essay that describes your goals in life. Remember to consider not only your educational or career aspirations but your personal and emotional goals as well. *Suggested writing focus:* gerunds and infinitives following verbs (for example, "I would like *to live* . . ." or "I can imagine *working* . . .").
6. In most cultures, colors have symbolic meanings. For example, red might signify anger; green might signify life. In a paragraph or an essay, reflect on the significance of a color (or various colors) in your culture. Use detailed examples to support your ideas. *Suggested writing focus:* sentence completeness and sentence structure.
7. If you could be invisible for a day, where would you go and what would you do? Write a paragraph or an essay in which you

describe your intentions or desires. *Suggested writing focus:* conditional sentences.

8. Visit an art museum or gallery and spend a few minutes looking closely at a piece of art that interests you. If that is not convenient, look around your campus for a painting or statue. Write a paragraph or an essay describing the work of art in detail. *Suggested writing focus:* articles or prepositions.

9. Sit down near a busy place on campus (or any other place you spend much of your time). Take a few minutes to observe the people and things around you. Write a paragraph or an essay describing what you see. *Suggested writing focus:* adjectives and adjective clauses.

10. Skim through the editorials or advice columns of a newspaper or magazine. Choose one that interests you. In a paragraph or a brief essay, write a summary of the article, making sure to include the author's main idea. *Suggested writing focus:* understanding main ideas.

11. In a well-organized essay, discuss the advantages (or disadvantages) of living with a roommate. Include a thesis statement and at least three supporting paragraphs. *Suggested writing focus:* thesis and support.

12. In a well-organized essay, discuss the negative impacts of a particular invention that is usually considered positive (such as the cell phone or the computer). *Suggested writing focus:* paragraph development.

13. In a well-organized essay, compare your personality to the personality of a close friend. (Who is more introverted, for example? Who takes more risks?) *Suggested writing focus:* using transitions between ideas.

14. Think about a social problem that bothers you or a social issue that you feel strongly about. In a well-organized essay, discuss the problem or issue and explain what should be done to improve the situation. Use information from two or three sources. Document your sources with in-text citations and include a works cited page. *Suggested writing focus:* citing sources in MLA style (see "citing sources" in the MLA section of your handbook).

15. Most colleges in the United States value critical thinking over memorization (see E1-b). In a well-organized essay, compare the negative aspects and positive aspects of these two ways of learning and then explain which one you think is preferable. Ask two friends or classmates what they think. Use their responses and your own reasons as evidence to support your position. Be sure to integrate the words or ideas of others into your essay. *Suggested writing focus:* integrating sources (see "integrating sources" in the MLA section of your handbook).

Answers to exercises

EXERCISE E1–1, page E-40

1. When she got home, Mina realized that she had forgotten to buy staples while she was out.
2. Martin Luther King Jr., the famous orator and civil rights activist, delivered his famous "I Have a Dream" speech on August 28, 1963.
3. David has played [or has been playing] soccer for the last fifteen years.
4. Mangoes, which originally grew only in Asia, now grow in the Eastern and Western Hemispheres.
5. Correct
6. Alexander Fleming discovered penicillin while he was working at a hospital in London.
7. Moving to a new country often causes people to change their lifestyles.
8. Although anthropologists do not know exactly when the first calendar was invented, they have evidence that solar calendars have existed for at least six thousand years.
9. When they moved here, my husband and his brother opened a small restaurant.
10. Professors in the United States often require their students to work in groups.

EXERCISE E1–2, page E-41

1. Woody Guthrie was one of the best-known American folk singer–activists.
2. Born in 1912, Guthrie spent his early life surrounded by music in his small hometown of Okema, Oklahoma.
3. Before his twentieth birthday, he moved to Texas, where he attempted to start a career as a musician.
4. Correct
5. Guthrie and his family moved west to California along with many other Texans and Oklahomans who found employment as farmworkers.
6. While he was traveling, he was exposed to the harsh treatment the migrant workers received.
7. By the time Guthrie arrived in California, he had developed a deep sense of resentment for the rich owners who exploited poor farmworkers.
8. He began writing and singing more songs about workers' rights and political protest, including his most famous song, "This Land Is Your Land."
9. He continued writing songs with a political message for the rest of his life and motivated many other popular folk and rock singers to carry on his legacy.
10. Today, Guthrie's music lives on in younger generations of people who feel inspired by his words.

EXERCISE E1–3, page E-41

When Julie visited the museum yesterday, she learned about the life cycle of the butterfly. The scientist at the museum explained the typical process: A butterfly, like all other insects, begins its life as an egg. When the egg hatches, a caterpillar emerges. The caterpillar spends its short life eating leaves on its host plant, growing larger in preparation for its transformation. After about two weeks, the caterpillar attaches itself to a stem and forms a chrysalis, a type of shell that protects it while it changes into a butterfly. After it is finished growing inside the chrysalis, the butterfly emerges. It rests on a leaf or stem while its wings dry and become stronger. When its wings become strong enough, it flies away.

EXERCISE E1–4, page E-42

Haley: Good morning, Professor Weil. May I ask you for some advice about my course work?

Professor Weil: Sure, Haley. What can I help you with?

H: I would like to change my major. I'm enrolled as a biology major now, but I am not as interested in science as I thought I would be.

P: I see. What major are you thinking of?

H: Since I am very good at math, I think I would like to be a business major.

P: That's a good idea, but can you do well in classes that don't involve math?

H: I think so. Which courses must I take besides math?

P: You will have to take some communications and writing courses.

H: I can do that. I will go to the registrar and select my courses. Thank you, Professor Weil!

EXERCISE E1–5, page E-42

Most people think of a trash bin as a finishing point rather than a starting point. However, a recycling bin can be the start of a new life for a piece of paper. After paper is put into an office bin, it is shipped to a recycling center, where it is sorted into types: office paper, cardboard, or colored paper. After it is sorted, it is sent to a paper mill, where it is chopped into dry pulp. The pulp is then mixed with water to form a wet substance called "slurry." The slurry is sent through a screen, which removes little bits of excess materials such as glue, plastic, or staples. After it goes through the screen, the slurry is rinsed again to remove inks. Then the slurry goes through a machine that makes the paper fibers grow bigger. Next the slurry is watered down and placed on a screen, where it is pressed into long, thin sheets and dried on heated rollers. The dried sheets are rolled up and shipped off to other companies where they are processed and made into the paper products we use every day.

EXERCISE E1–6, page E-43

1. If the governor is reelected, she will not raise the income tax.
2. I could not park my car next to the library because all of the spaces were taken.
3. Sadly, a cure for AIDS has not been found yet.
4. The book that we have to buy for our ecology class is not very expensive.
5. I tried to make a photocopy, but the copier was not functioning properly.
6. Sunnie did not come with us to the football game last Saturday.
7. Although Omar does not like to drive in traffic, he likes to race cars on the weekends.
8. Snow leopards are not extinct, but they are on the endangered species list.
9. Kim could not find lychees [or any lychees] at the supermarket because they are not very common in the United States.
10. I was disappointed that I didn't know the woman's name.

EXERCISE E1–7, page E-43

1. If Deborah had arrived earlier, she might have found a better parking space.
2. I'll buy you a soda if you come to the cafeteria with me.
3. Correct
4. Correct
5. If I were a famous actor, I would move to Bel Aire and buy a mansion.
6. If you use aloe on a burn, you can reduce the chances of developing a scar.
7. You will have to pay late charges if you don't return your movie rental on time.
8. Unless the Security Council agrees, the UN will not send peacekeeping troops to war-torn countries.
9. When Rosa left for college every September, she closed her summer gardening business. *Or* When Rosa leaves for college every September, she closes her summer gardening business.
10. If Kevin were here with us today, he would be enjoying himself.

EXERCISE E1–8, page E-44

When I was young, my family and I went on an annual camping trip in the canyons of the southwestern United States. One summer, I convinced my family to take a tour of several canyons: the Grand Canyon, Bryce Canyon, and Canyonlands National Park. I remember being amazed at each stop along the way. I loved looking up at the twisting towers of red rock, wondering how they had avoided falling down in the last several thousand years. (I can recall thinking that some might fall over if someone in the canyon sneezed a little too hard.) Even at that young age, I sensed the power of these remarkable landmarks and understood the spell that they had held over so many generations of residents and visitors. In my heart, I promised to go back to the canyons every year. Though I never planned to give up my promise, the commitments of adulthood have prevented me from taking annual trips back to the canyons. I miss visiting the red rocks on a regular basis, but I still manage to go back to the Southwest every few years. Breathing in the high desert air while gazing up at the red rock towers never ceases to refresh and rejuvenate me.

EXERCISE E2–1, page E-44

When I was a child, I did not like to work. Every time my parents asked me to clean my room or study for my classes, I always found an excuse. Sometimes I would pretend that I was too tired; other times I would pretend that I had simply forgotten their request. Most of the time, however, I would try to approach the situation logically, arguing that since my older brother was stronger and had more life experience, he should be responsible for most of the household chores.

However, when I started college, my life changed. I realized that to become the successful college student I wanted to be, I would have to take control of my life, change my bad habits, and act responsibly. Now I am no longer the boy my parents knew when I was a child. I wake up early, exercise, and go to school. I am never late to my classes, and I always turn my assignments in on time. Although I am still far from perfect, I try to help others whenever I can. Whenever someone needs me, particularly at school or at home, I never try to hide as I did when I was just a boy.

EXERCISE E2–2, page E-45

It is common to think that being the oldest child in a family has the most privileges. However, there are several advantages to being the youngest child, too. First, it is important to note that by the time the youngest child is born, the parents have already had experience as parents. They know how to care for a newborn, and they tend to be more relaxed. Second, the youngest child has the opportunity to learn how to stay out of trouble. If the older children get into trouble, it is easy for the youngest child to learn from the older children's mistakes. A third advantage of being the youngest child is that in many cases, the youngest gets extra attention from the older siblings. It is not unusual to see older siblings taking care of their younger siblings at school or protecting them from bullies.

EXERCISE E2–3, page E-45

Possible revisions:

1. Coming to the United States changed more than my address. It changed the direction of my career.
2. My life here in Gainesville is different from the life that I lived in Bolivia.
3. Correct
4. I attended a culinary school, which was the best in Bolivia, and I was offered the chance to study for a short time in the United States.
5. When I first came, I met other students who had different majors.
6. Correct
7. Jin helped me realize the importance of having business experience.
8. I learned that although I enjoyed being a chef, I didn't want to be a chef without business knowledge.
9. I decided to stay a bit longer in the United States, where I could study international business.
10. Someday I will combine both interests and start my own chain of specialized restaurants, which I hope to build all over the world.

EXERCISE E2–4, page E-46

1. I have never seen a player hit a baseball so hard.
2. Sue cooked the soup very slowly so that the vegetables would be tender.
3. Correct
4. After I finished my workout, I carefully stretched my tender muscles.
5. The professor seemed surprised that the class finished the exam so quickly.
6. After I read the user manual, I easily installed the new hard drive.
7. My mother always told me that she loved all her children equally.
8. As soon as I got the keys to my new car, I drove my friends everywhere.
9. The government found out that the company manufactured the drug illegally.
10. Although she had a difficult time in the past, this year she very easily won the gold medal in cross-country skiing.

EXERCISE E3–1, page E-46

1. When people move to a new place, they definitely have to go through some changes.
2. The temperature dropped twenty degrees in a half hour yesterday.

3. Some governments help couples who have more than two children by giving them health insurance.
4. When people are too busy, they sometimes forget to eat dinner.
5. Students are exposed to new experiences when they move to a new country.
6. I chose to have a small family so that I could give my children sufficient attention.
7. Marco became more familiar with nature when he studied in the rain forests of Brazil.
8. Let me give you some advice: Buy your books early.
9. A common effect of culture shock is loneliness.
10. Because our school doesn't allow cars within the campus gates, I walk from my parking spot to the place where I need to go.

EXERCISE E3–2, page E-47

Heifer International is a nonprofit organization that provides animals to poor farmers and families around the world. The organization was started in the 1940s by a man named Dan West, a relief worker who gave people food during times of crisis. West realized that he could help people even more by giving them animals that could supply food — such as milk and cheese — for several years. He wanted to help people for the long term, and he wanted to help them have pride in themselves. Now Heifer serves communities in more than one hundred countries around the world. Its mission is to help families by providing some animals that the families can use to support themselves or start small businesses.

EXERCISE E3–3, page E-47

Possible revisions:

A greeting is the way that a person addresses or acknowledges another person when the two meet. Types of greetings vary in different countries. People in Japan often prefer to greet nonverbally, with a bow and a smile. An African would likely greet a fellow African with a handshake. For the Maori people of New Zealand, the most common greeting is the *hongi*, which involves rubbing noses. In Poland, a kiss on each cheek is customary; but the Dutch custom is to kiss the right cheek, then the left, and then the right again. A traveler to another country would be wise to learn the greetings expected by its people.

EXERCISE E4–1, page E-47

1. confusing
2. tiring
3. boring
4. working
5. fascinating
6. handwritten, typed
7. satisfied
8. hand-painted
9. cleaning
10. peeled

EXERCISE E5–1, page E-48

1. Does your dance class start on Monday or Wednesday?
2. Correct
3. As soon as Fiona moved into her dorm room, she put a poster of Einstein on the wall for inspiration.
4. My books are a little dusty because they were packed away in the garage for a year.
5. Dr. Horn is taking his students to Ghana for a study trip in early June.
6. My grandmother was born in Los Angeles, but my grandfather was born in Albuquerque.
7. My fraternity brothers like to play loud music on the street in front of our building.
8. My exam begins in two hours, but I'm not nervous at all.
9. Correct
10. Bret finished writing his term paper right at midnight.

EXERCISE E5–2, page E-48

1. I have trouble concentrating on my homework when my roommate is around.
2. The senator was skilled at delaying controversial votes.
3. I'm not worried about our verbs test on Wednesday.
4. While Ellie proofread the group's report, Sam and Tomi worked on the presentation slides.
5. Correct
6. The solution consists of sodium and water.
7. I was afraid to board the plane because I'm not accustomed to traveling alone.
8. Shea remained devoted to the teachings of his martial arts master.
9. You can always count on Carole to help out when the office gets busy.
10. Correct

Index